CARRYING

THE

WORLD

Also by Maxine Beneba Clarke

Foreign Soil
The Hate Race

Published in Australia and New Zealand in 2016
by Hachette Australia
(an imprint of Hachette Australia Pty Limited)
Level 17, 207 Kent Street, Sydney NSW 2000
www.hachette.com.au

10 9 8 7 6 5 4 3 2 1

Copyright © Maxine Beneba Clarke 2016

This book is copyright. Apart from any fair dealing for the purposes of private study, research, criticism or review permitted under the *Copyright Act 1968*, no part may be stored or reproduced by any process without prior written permission. Enquiries should be made to the publisher.

National Library of Australia
Cataloguing-in-Publication data:

Clarke, Maxine Beneba, author.
Carrying the world/Maxine Beneba Clarke.

978 0 7336 3640 0 (pbk)

Australian poetry – 21st century.

A821.4

Cover design and illustration by Allison Colpoys
Text design by Bookhouse, Sydney
Typeset in 12/16.5 pt Bembo Pro by Bookhouse, Sydney
Printed and bound in Australia by McPherson's Printing Group

The excerpt from 'Advance Australia Fair' that appears on page 115 is reproduced with the permission of the Australian Government.

The paper this book is printed on is certified against the Forest Stewardship Council® Standards. McPherson's Printing Group holds FSC chain of custody certification SG5-COC-004121. FSC promotes environmentally responsible, socially beneficial and economically viable management of the world's forests.

for Robert,
hell, look what we made

CONTENTS

armageddon	1
bed 87	3
brown	5
bundaberg was not a flood	7
carrying the world	9
confetti	14
dead poets society	16
delilah	18
demerara sugar	21
disappeared	54
even if it gets to 104°	57
fairytale	66
get real	70
ghetto gentry	72
gil scott-heron is on parole	77
if: a rewrite	81
i is the revolution	85
in karikatur australisch deutsch	89
jack	103

little michael	106
mali	109
marngrook	113
megan	121
mistah school teachah	124
nothing here needs fixing	127
plantation rumour	147
ryan gosling and the new feminism	150
sewn shut	152
show me a girl, at five	154
show us where you're publishing	159
skin	162
speakers' corner	163
subtext	165
summer	167
the end of the affair	168
unmiracle	171
we want poetry back	174
what are you going to say	177
acknowledgements	181

armageddon

i / refused somebody a dollar today
and now / i think he
might've really needed it

was there armageddon in
the way / my head shook
knowing yeah / i had no coins
but there was five dollars curled
right up there in my pocket

he didn't smell so good
i was reading some paper that
might've cost more than he
even asked me for / i can't
remember / and besides
i / don't really want to
think about what i did

he wore threadbare converse
fingernails black
like mushroom undersides

armageddon

he might've been asking / for
the only meal in two days / or
a bus fare home / to his daughter

i / didn't think about how hard
it would've been for him to ask
in the first place
it was the tail end
of a rough day / and i
wanted him to move on

he had already approached everybody
on the station / was i his
final chance at a bed tonight

the forecast says it might
get down to zero / out there

and me / i might've been
somebody's / armageddon

bed 87

november to march
every year for five
i was just another hospital dinner lady
serving scrambled eggs on the breakfast tray-line
lining breakfast trays with blunt knives
blunt-knived-to-bleeding all the time
(those were some summer holidays of mine)

it cost money to get educated
and educated was what i was going to be
not just another pink-aproned tea run
offering lukewarm nerada and sara lee

this was a means to be free

the old man in bed eighty-seven said he liked me
that my morning smile was like being in heaven
and heaven was just where he wanted to be

said he had to eat to live
and if he didn't eat they'd feed him
that the worst news i could bring
was stone-cold toast and half-frozen corned beef
i was never going to say *it's spreading*

when he saw it was me at the door
we both bled a sigh of relief

i was just another hospital dinner lady
serving scrambled eggs on the breakfast tray-line
while both of us bided our time

brown

    sometimes
bronzed terracotta mahogany
    i wake
burnished hazelnut beige
    with rope
scarlet brown cedar
tanned sandstone
oaked earth
and red-rusted caramel gold
    round my neck
chocolate
raw umber
scorched hazel
    dripping
burnt macadamian cream
    sweat
walnut sienna
and mapled sahara
ripe olive on dark aubergine
    out of
earth clayed treacle
    breath

brown

>*dog at my*
> honeyed tree-sap
> *heels*

>*bleeding but*
> carmine coffee bean
> *free*

>*afraid to*
> stained pine sunset
> *dream*

bundaberg was not a flood
(after ntozake shange's *mood indigo*)

it hasn't always been this way

we are drinking in the company
of men who made the rain

six-point-zero / on the richter scale
forty-four centigrade
condensation on the window pane

tsunami on the way

sandbags / on the coast of new orleans
braced against the oklahoma winds
cowering from the florida breeze
running like river / from the nagasaki sea

blonde as bone sheep carcass
over dry / drought-cracked barren land
bovine leather slack
on lean spare ribs

the canning factories are closing down

bundaberg was not a flood

dams drained down to silt
swelling through flash flood
from acid rain

it hasn't always been this way:
we are drinking in the company
of men who blew the richter scale
elvis was not a firecraft
bundaberg was not a flood
new orleans was not a hurricane
as i knew them
both *sandy* and *katrina* / they
were mid-seventies white girl names

it hasn't always been this way

encyclopaedia britannica
was not a glossary of fault-line fates

haiti / now she was not a quake
it hasn't always been this way

we are drinking in the company of
men who blew the richter scale

carrying the world

the rocking chair strains
under weight of it all
the ole woman's frail
but she's carrying the world
as she knits one purl
she knit knits one purl

her left eye's shut bung
since glaucoma came knocking
for a home / the arthritis creaks
she try and beat it back / but
the thing refuse to leave
and that's all she needs
to accompany the rage
as she knit purl sway
she knit knit purl sway

she nod nod
and smile
at neighbour's children
wagoning on by
all pigtails and cheek
yam-bellied and buck-teethed
she nod nod

carrying the world

and smile
nod nod / and smile
an ole woman / holding up the sky
on a porch / in a brixton street

y'all don't know her name
so let's call her Black History

she's weary
travelled continents of hate
her head aches
she had her skull cracked
on portobello lane
in the riots of 1958
white policeman bailed her up
and said *lubra / there ain't no use
trying to be brave*
and then he
clubbed the nigger round head
to keep himself *out of harm's way*

carrying the world

as the young girl fell
the road spun dizzy round
and everywhere
a race war raged

the rocking chair strains
under weight of it all
the ole woman's frail
but she's carrying the world
as she knits one purl
she knit knits one purl

witnessed her own children
take up arms against each other
blood brother decapitating brother
her hutu first daughter
betrayed her tutsi third son / her
kikuyu uncle slayed whole forests
into dusty kenyan plain / her
arteries flood red
like the killing fields of the congo / her
heart beat has slowed
to the drumming of the igbo's djembe

carrying the world

and the rocking chair
and the rocking chair
and the rocking chair strains
under weight of it all
the ole girl grows weary
of shouldering the world

being shackled under deck
      knit purl
hurled up overboard
      knit purl
being hauled to auction block
      knit purl
broken in the fields
      knit purl
being sold down the mississip—
and the knitting needles go
click
click
click

carrying the world

an ole woman weeps
an ole woman weeps in a rocking chair
on a porch
on a brixton street
y'all don't know her name
so let's call her Black History

confetti

six slim lip-syncing years *of him*
squeezed in / to his
two-year-old sister's
pink / empire line dress

angelina ballerina gloves
smoothed lovingly to elbow
matted curly red wig
perched / lopsided on this head

as if he can't decide
between little orphan annie
and ageing miss havisham

either way

this kid does old-time
raggedy-down-on-her-luck-diva
believably well

a brief interval
to re-apply his sweaty
strawberry chapstick:

the closest his mum will let him get
until the judo master tells her he can kick

mum stands by the clothes line
transfixed / resigned
empty cane basket at feet
as the light / filtered
by silky oak leaves
scatters a showgirl's
confetti

dead poets society

and when you go
people you never knew
will send *oh captain / my captains*
into eternal cyber circulation

and when you go / they
will all proclaim that
when you said / *carpe diem*
seize the day / you
changed the world / or their soul
or an entire generation

and when you go
when you go
they'll crank another print run / re-run
your movies until dawn

and in the end / they'll always say
well / she never eclipsed
that first role / or book / or exhibition / or album

or else in the end / they'll s*ay / such*
a shame / it just doesn't make the least shred of sense

his last role / or book / or exhibition / or album
it really was his best

and when i go
i will go to this darkness
between / the crimson carpets

here / where art
does not live
on art alone

and i / its feeder
have faltered

delilah

delilah / you were dark
like me and africa

a beautiful continent
easy to corrupt

ruined by a man / you
could never hope to defeat

and left to burn
when / by some miracle
you did

delilah / nobody cared
what happened behind
closed doors / with the body
of a brute who can't bleed
bruised against yours

a fierce black woman
beating your way forward
in a world made
for mythical white men

delilah

sick of swollen purple eyes
washing bloody fingerprints
from curved thighs / scared
but ready to try anything

delilah / you were the first
supreme / brown-skinned
sunday-schoolers everywhere
committed judges 16:6 to memory
and said *damn / she's cool*
i want to be like her

conjured you / in the churchyard
with tina turner legs
a james brown howl
and jackson five hair
turning rivers / to moonshine
discipled by doo-wop girls

you were cake-walked across water
to gob-smacked fishermen
turning loaves to cornbread
and fish / to fried chitterling

delilah

you better believe / your
trials meant *something*

before chaka kahn
etta james / and missy e
you were *delilah*:
the original supreme

demerara sugar

i
my mother clamours in
her kitchen / with
a loudness / reserved / for
those accustomed to living
alone / her bare feet
thud the floorboards
she jangles the cutlery / clang
into the stainless steel sink

two rooms away / my
children turn
tangle-sheeted metres
of summer holiday
nanna's-house heat

    are you all organised
    for the trip
which in old country
is really saying
    chile / ye still don't seem te know
    wat all which way is up

demerara sugar

absentminded / i pick
at the tired cane placemat
the weaving inadvertently
unravels / my mother
dries her hands / on red
checked flannelette

>   *your grandmother*

she says

>   *was warned not to marry my father*
>   *if you go asking questions*
>   *this is something you just*
>   *might come across*

>   *her own father / begged*
>   *her not to marry him / but*
>   *she was in love / already*
>   *with child / a beautiful*
>   *strong-willed girl*

>   *they were notorious*
>   *the critchlow men*

everyone in plaisance / knew
what happened / to their women

i am still with shock

sit unmoving
sit unmoving

against the now
quiet room

ii
i know what all the aunties
gwan be saying

this niece of mine a-coming say
she going voyage west africa
some writer say she trace
our lineage / sure
along the coast

they saying / huh

she going old country
what / she gon feed the chain
back through the black
atlantic / she gon mark lines
through tottenham plaisance
walthamstow jonestown

they saying don't she know
there things we ole folks
don't talk about / things she
herself has only just begun to know
this sister niece second cousin once
removed / from some country / huh
where was it now she from?

waltzing in like / she got
some kinda right in asking all
these things

she wanna feed the chain
back through the black atlantic

say she digging up / to find
where from we come

huh / what she made of
what she made of

see her face when history
come a-call

she reeling
oh / she reeling

and our skeletons
they floating low

iii
house closed up
power points switched to off
stray food tucked away in
tupperware containers pot plants entrusted
to friends blinds pulled all the way
across car packed in

demerara sugar

the driveway
waiting

i water / one last time

melbourne summer evenings the
sun stays to fight off night:
flails angry fists of white
yellow heat

the full-force hose
on our ragged still-green tomato crop
zucchini flower dusty rhubarb stalk
almost seeding kale

strange

strange / this january
has brought a mushroom soil:
compost-black

and heavy
like molasses

the apple tree
which last year bore riddled fruit
stretches red-red-green offerings
on myriad gnarled arms

kids already
in the car / we reverse
out the driveway

out of time / leave behind
the fallen fruit

at forty-one degrees / and
holding / the tumbled apples
will split their skin

on parched / browning grass
their sourness will crystallise

demerara sugar

black and heavy
black and heavy like

molasses

iv
to reach the empire we cut
backward through the day / hanging
thick outside the round-edged window
pane / there is dawn
the slow rising of the light
around us / the almost-blindness
white noise aviating behind
the eyelids / at times the altitude
is too much / to brace
against

     the kids pick at foil-lidded meals
sleep fitfully in their seats / wake often

wake always / wake
asking about

       journey's end

v
my sister / who lives here now
at heathrow / smiling
the kids run / grin up at auntie

outside / london
creeps through our fibres

my dead guyanese grandfather
the one my nanna wasn't meant / to marry

is here with us already
and a-whispering

dem tell ye / bring ye warmest
is very cold / but ye lived

ye entire life under de sun
an my god / my god chile
ye realise / ye hav nat known real cold

he say
on de docks / chile
on de docks ye si dem tremblin-knee
children wearin everytin dem own
six pair-a underwear widdem tights
on top / an two pair-a trouser
one go on over de other

he a-whispering
four t-shirt three thin cotton jumper
ye tinking: what fresh hell is dis
what de hell is dis mother country
te which wi come

my southern hemisphere children huddle
wide-eyed with surprise
they did not know / until now
what real cold was

we sleep fitfully / crowded in one room
at my mother's younger sister's house
in ilford / the children wake asking
about departure / asking
about home
      asking often

vi
coffee

    on the docks
of west india quay

chill wind / outside
the london museum

thawing palms / around cardboard cup
water still / against this
winter

      bitterness

demerara sugar

planks still sticky with
raisins banana rum / still
gritty with tea tobacco rice

my god
the *sugar* warehouse

it was busy here
               in arrivals

the workers
they called this place
blood alley

burlap sacks rough heavy ripped
open dock workers' backs
plasma hands / unloaded
their wares / unloaded the west
indies / unloaded africa
unloaded *us*

sweet splintered ground
uneven with granule spill

i was not made for this
            bitterness
i was maid

            for this
            bitterness

inside the docks museum
print scrolls the wall

you will be taken from your home
will not keep your name will
not speak your language you
will be violated not able to keep
your children will have no
property you will be sold

it would be best not
to look / at that screen
i tell my son / *this is just*
an exhibit anyway

demerara sugar

i am not a good liar
even at two years old
he could already read my face
and now he is nine / a fellow
traveller / a light-skinned brown
boy / already old enough
for the big house

and they would have him

along one wall / a slave chain hangs
this is not a replica the sign says

lift it up the sign says
and feel how heavy it is

my son looks / at me
like he might be coming down
with something

this is a london winter
he / was not made to weather

my throat hurts / mama
he says

the numbers
run aground the
black-black tally-ship wall

departed cape castle arrived
jamaica departed gambia
arrived demerara departed
bance island arrived barbados

hundreds are the unarrived
hundreds are the missing

they unload their
wares / unload the
west indies / unload
africa / unload *us*

demerara sugar

blood alley they called this place

my throat hurts my son says
    my throat

vii
the train to liverpool winds through
green meadows past cedar brick houses
square white-rimmed windows
straight-backed girls in
equestrian helmets quaint villages with
spindly trees thick fog hovers over
and holds

    trains pubs ornate finishes
concrete municipal buildings
sandstone facade

penny lane

on the beatles trail
all the locals nod and say

as if for sure they know
our tourist game

down water street
my son and daughter
in snow boots and kathmandu
past west africa house / across
the gorge / down to the waterfront
hunched / against the wind and blain

penny lane

zero degrees
another portside coffee cart
maritime hot chocolate
and the woman who serves us says
    snow has just been forecast
says *your children they are not in school*
looks at me
looks at me / the way they all do

demerara sugar

it is summer holidays / where we come from
i say / she is wondering where from
we possibly came

at the international museum
of slavery / i
plug the children in
ipad / headphone splitter / box
of skittles / to share

the first booth wraps all the
way around waves slam on
the ship hull wailing buries
me beneath the black atlantic
there is blood everywhere
are screams everywhere
the black atlantic
pushes me beneath

and i can't breathe
jesus / i can't breathe

simulated slave ship
the placard says

demerara sugar

351 chained in
14 metres by 8 and
the journey / it took
49 days

heartache the madness the
mama up on the morning of the auction / the
being sure they are not crying the braiding hair
dress them nice you hear
be sure they fetch a good price
big rations if your pickney fetch a few
maybe you could work up in the big house
bet you'd like that you'd like that wouldn't you
well be sure they don't cling on or wail see

metal instruments in glass cases
branding iron remnants of dead flesh
metal muzzle should you speak *out of turn*
tongue cutter
chain gang coffle

i shackled him in wooden
stocks by the hands neck and
feet so as to immobilise him

demerara sugar

he was taken out to the field
and painted with molasses from head to toe

the runaway was left to lie
there for several weeks

this is not a replica
original item
testimonial

my children they are hungry / the
skittles have run out / and they
have come to find me

mama / mama
my daughter is saying

she can't see me
but i am standing right here
mama / mama
she can't see me / right here

in green meadows past cedar brick houses
square white-rimmed windows
straight-backed girls in
equestrian helmets quaint villages with
spindly trees / a thick fog hovering over
and holding

in heartache the madness / the
mama up on the morning
of the auction
the 14 by 8 by 49
by 351 chained

i am standing
my god
right here
on liverpool's
penny lane

viii
the restaurant on the top floor is decked out
like old-time cruise / amongst the pillars

demerara sugar

we order bolognese / fizzy lemonade
and fancy four-pound meat

cary grant and paul robeson all
the stars adorn the walls

transatlantic dining
*   the menu says*

a smorgasbord
guaranteed / to evoke
the ocean liners

of yesteryear

ix
black brixton
six celsius degrees and falling

i heard a whisper / the food market
still bears the markings

where from they bolted
the slave pen in

black brixton
and my history / huh
humming / through stone

the children chase
pigeons round the concrete
and green / my daughter
not yet five /　already
outrunning her brother
at half his size

    windrush square

is paved outside
the black british archives:
a monument
glory be / to the first
of our arrived

demerara sugar

but the chill wind she
cutting through / this
dead empty space

like we nothing

black brixton
six celsius degrees

and falling

the empire windrush
she got secrets / that ship
secrets so big i don't
know what to do with

secrets it may not
be wise to tell

(be sure you ask / before she dock
in jamaica what all cargo
she been ferrying)

black brixton
and falling

inside the archives / photo reels
shows the rebels of railton road / adorned
oh yeah / in black panther *finery*
anger / flares
boots and rude

black brixton

black brixton
six celsius degrees

but the chill wind / she
cutting through / this
dead empty space

like we nothing

this my history / huh
humming through stone

demerara sugar

x
your great uncle buddy
he always was a handsome man
all done up right
streamlined jacket
shined shoes waxed-up hair
with just that little lean
on the side

and damn / the way he carry

your uncle buddy
he was a damn sharp black
ladies'-man dandy
weren't no girl on the block could
say no to him

you go talk to uncle buddy
your nanna gone
rest her sweet soul
but he her closest brother
he gon know it all

he be what / bout eighty-five now

used to pick me up
in my saturday finery
at your nana millie's house
i was all of six
maybe even five and
we would go a-visiting
to his girlfriends' – *plural* – houses

much less suspicious with
some cute lolly-bag kid
hanging round

yeah

go see buddy
you're gonna like him
he give you a story
hell / he give you ten
he a devil / yeah
a god-handsome devil
that waxed-up
with a just that little
lean on the side man

xi
that can't be right
that is almost
one hundred pounds
      i say

the woman behind the long-haul desk frowns
a tad annoyed / a little bit
yeah i know / it's outrageous
but what are you going
to do about it anyway

one adult / and one child
      i say
my son and i
board and wait

birmingham is always further away
than you thought it was
there is something slow
about the journey / something
outside of meantime / even
slicing atmosphere / inside
a red virgin bullet train

birmingham is further away
than you know

off to see my great uncle buddy
and his second / maybe even
third / i don't know / but
what a nice english lady
she turns out / wife

uncle buddy / is sharp as tack
only sometimes / he calls me
by my mother's name
sometimes he mistakes me for her
don't think i mind though
i really don't mind that

your grandfather
      uncle buddy says
he used to say he would never go back
to that place – to plaisance guyana
not even if somebody paid him

demerara sugar

the way he would say it / my dear
'that place' like it was haunted
by some evil jumbie of a thing

my great mama
somehow we swing round to her

uncle buddy / all i know is
all i got told / she died young

i was three years old / dear
uncle buddy says / *when my mama got sick*

they took her to the hospital
shortly after that / she laid down and died
poor thing / she was tired i suppose
only thirty-eight / and she'd already
birthed eight of us / my mama just
got tired / i guess

my son is perched
on the faded sofa rest
ipad on knee / recording his mama
and his great great uncle
chasing history down

demerara sugar

tall glass of lemonade
sloshing over / in his hand

it is too cold for lemonade
      i think
and then
she just laid down and died
i don't know
that just doesn't sound right

it is too cold for lemonade
lemonade is too dangerous

blood sugar
blood sugar
the way it brews so badly
in our family blood
almost all the aunties this side
got it now

sugar / bet you that's what it was
demerara sugar
bet you anything
it took uncle buddy's ma

demerara sugar

four hundred years on
demerara is still trying
to kill us all
some evil jumbie of a thing

birmingham has turned out close
birmingham is closer than i knew

xii
on the last night
my sister and i
we fight in her
finsbury park
kitchen

my daughter / she sleeps london
to dubai / her brother / he sleeps
dubai to melbourne

me / i bleary-eye home

demerara sugar

heat climbing
to forty-one degrees
and holding

black molasses

black molasses

all the tumbled apples
split their skin

disappeared

just last year
another young black man was disappeared

you forget his name
or did you know it

roughed up by cops in flemington
his body surfaced
crushed and bruised
on the yarra – or perhaps
it was the maribyrnong – banks

nobody could really say
what happened

sweet jesus

disappeared

another black man

remember liep gony
stabbed to death while riding home:

disappeared

a kid coming back
from his fast food job
on just another ordinary
black boy day

liep gony lived several suburbs from me
liep gony / was my kid too

in the news some short while
but nobody remembers him now
he was more than just a dead boy
but he was *just* a dead boy brown

the immigration minister
of the day / he said
these sudanese
have a real problem
with integration

a black kid did not come home that day
and that was his eulogy offering

back in june / back in june
a taxi driver / was attacked

disappeared

driving a handful of somebodies safely
– or so he thought –
home from the melbourne night
go back to where you came from they said
he was an indian man
they were white boys
they had baseball bats
theirs were no uncertain terms

yet another good-bloke copper
chasing yet another koori kid
to yet another death
yet another good-bloke copper
chasing yet another koori kid
to yet another death
yet another koori kid
dead

it happened

disappeared
yeah / it happened

yet again

even if it gets to 104°

i
back in birmingham alabama
hate blew up little brown church girls
in taffeta and acapella

not yet halfway through their lives

not yet halfway down the communion stairs
and already halfway to heaven

can i get a witness

there is gunpowder
in the house of adam

at the emanuel episcopal church
there stands a pockmarked pulpit

cabernet stains on window glass

hate disguised himself
and smiled in fellowship

the good christian people
they welcomed him
with open arms

can i get a witness

there is gunpowder
in the house of god

nothing suspicious to report
in ferguson missouri
they are saying
electrical faults
in knoxville tennessee
they are saying
no sign of arson
in charlotte north carolina
they are saying
cause undetermined
in florida (tallahassee)

can i get a witness

even if it gets to 104°

the black churches
they are burning

they keep saying
no cause for alarm

but there is fire
can i get a witness

there is fire
in the house of god

ii
and still we grow them
bones near buckling
coaxing our unborn
toward us with
bitter tea

our children's names
are revealed to us

even if it gets to 104°

sure as the moon
in the heavy pregnant night

they are all still breathing
they are all still loved
they arrive screaming
already lined in chalk

and still we grow them
bones near buckling
coaxing out
our unborn

iii
if your friends wanna play with water
down there in the park
i don't care how hot it is
even if it gets to 104 degrees
the moment they get out them
plastic squirter guns an start fillin up
at that fountain / just run
don't even stop to explain / just you

turn around an run all the way
home to me

someone passing by think
you got the real deal
pointed there

listen hear / black boys
got shot for less

if your car breaks down
even in the middle
of the motorway
leave it right there / baby
don't you flag nobody down for help

that thing ain't nothin but
a lump of clever metal anyway

or if you love the car too much
to let it go / then just you an your friends
you push it over to the side of the road

even if it gets to 104°

don't you flag nobody down

push it all the way on home
if you have to

it don't matter how your knees
feel like they gon buckle
or how people on the sidewalk
lookin at you funny

stares don't kill

stares don't kill you hear me
don't never flag no other car
down for help don't you never
flag no other car down

black boys been shot for less
and i want you comin home every single
night / baby

an if you runnin home
from playin water pistols at the park

or from leavin some car
that just broke down on you

if you ever runnin home
an somebody yell stop

for the love of jesus / chile
just stop / stop an put your hands in the air
stop an put your hands in the air
an get down on your knees an
don't make no sudden movements

yes sir an no sir or better still / yes officer
an no officer / yeah
even then / if you don't mean it

even if he got a gun pointed right at you
especially if he got a gun / baby
pointed right at you

do you hear me
do you hear me now

i don't care how hot it is
even if it gets to 104 degrees
you come back home to me

iv
that's his mama
over there in the black
the woman looking over

she wants to know
how you knew her son

can you give her that

the service is over
but you could stay
a while / and talk

did her son sit next to you
in english lit class / at school

even if it gets to 104°

do you live here in
the neighbourhood / was he
on your football
your toastmasters
or your swimming team

was the dead black boy
your mama's cleaner's son
say she think she seen you
somewhere before

did you work the check-out counter
at the sanford walmart too
could be you knew him
please / his mama looking over
and she deserves to hear

fairytale

the teacher reads snow white
in our fairytale
my daughter will scar herself
with household bleach tonight
crying mirror on the wall
erase this face as black as night

the beast is the head of the militia
beauty is an african child
he has her circumcised at five
and she weeps in the honeymoon bed

i / don't want to kiss a frog prince
or hope i turn to swan
gonna be like goldilocks
and help myself
don't tell me that it's wrong
call it colonisation
the bears i shoot
aren't civilised anyway
i'll grab the biggest
porridge bowl / and fire

fairytale

once upon a time
in a fairytale

a goose that laid a golden egg
was called a pregnant slave
the king's horses
and the king's men / sold
children down the mississip—
away / no matter how hard
mama cried / no handsome prince
or pumpkin coach came

i put the brothers in the grimm

in the grade three reading room
i / cut my little library card
in two / and said / *thank you
miss librarian / but black kids
don't do / hans christian anderson*

we were the hunted wolves
cowered down in grandma's
room / hiding from white hoods
that stained red while riding

fairytale

through the wood / black life
is not a children's book

disney says / *every little girl
would like to be either sleeping
beauty or cinderella* / well
i missed the tribal ball
slept for five hundred years
and woke to find my prince
had been lynched / rap
was king / and the continent
was dying

i am the match girl left
out in the cold / if i don't burn
this fiction down
it's not for want of trying

these tales come for our young
like rumpelstiltskin
till they believe they can
spin straw into record deals
slay the dragon
and claim the kingdom

fairytale

hands up / who
volunteers / to teach my
children happily ever
after / may not include
the servants / in the kitchen

get real

he says real poets don't wrestle
for silence / in beer-packed bars
echo words from / temple walls
or scream down the pews / of
churches / he says real poets
don't force you to listen / howl
it out on a street corner mic / slam
around the tennis / above the orders
before the band / he says get
the fuck out of here / who
do you think you are / why
don't you piss off before i—
real poets aren't in your face
aren't big / aren't black aren't
women / aren't young
and sure don't look like
that / real poets are PhDs bush
men / or working-class heroes
would a real poet / rock
that boat / march this street
wield a gun / or *mother
fuck* hecklers / like that
he says / nuh uh / i don't
think so / you ain't a poet

get real

wrong way sister / go back
shut the hell up / get off
turn the thing down / go
home and wait near the
letterbox slot / real poets go
all angst over that editorial
knock back / hang out in
libraries / sleep in squats
and starve for their art

real poets / don't have white-
collar jobs / stay up writing
all night cut their wrists
twice yearly / and eventually
they get it / right / he says
poet my arse / don't try to
fool me / real poets don't
believe in anything / except
poetry / and they certainly
do not stand / on the corner
of gertrude and smith
giving their work away
for free

ghetto gentry

no matter what city
west of the city
always gets a bad rap

they say *the streets*
are littered with rubbish
headscarves / brown bodies
no-good good-for-nothing
playing-hooky teens

from what the hell kind of
high school out there
could even teach them
the seven days of the week

beat-sneakers hung
from powerlines
and shop-keepers who refuse
to speak english / man
it's ironic even
calling it 'the west'

ghetto gentry

*little abu dhabi / dumpling-sweet
pork bun / i heard it's
really made from fat stray cat
bogans down and out
of their minds on crack
because white folks
who choose to live west
of the city / they have got
to be absolutely whack*

*blue eyes is like finding a syringe
in a bayside café pancake stack*

west of the city
always gets a bad rap

and still / when school gets out
the white kids head to
williamstown and yarraville
where working class has been upcycled
reclaimed by *friends of the earth*
and collectives so-named
certifiably organic fruit
and veg / and fair trade

ghetto gentry

coffee shops with homemade
vegan banana bread:

when it is a white ghetto
it has been *gentrified*
when it is a brown ghetto
we are *disadvantaged*

right

but the real parties
good food / and folk who
dance undrunk / they happen
over on the brown side

bring yarraville over here to us
we will show them
who their neighbours are
and what the real ghetto
gentry does

hoist me up the fence
point those ghetto-blasters
to the maribyrnong sky

we are gonna decolonise
the airways over geelong road
tonight

history speaks / of berlin
and palestine / but on this
stolen land / suburban highways
are race-dividing lines:
vicious voting clusters for
anti-immigration lies

for some / where you live
is not *where* you are / but *who*
and three suburbs that way
an extra hundred thou
will guarantee
your neighbour's hue

but we move fast

there is no mistaking that / there
is no mistaking that
there is no escaping that

ghetto gentry

no matter what suburb
in no matter what city

west of the city
always gets a bad rap

gil scott-heron is on parole

gil scott-heron / is on parole
    revolution
gil scott-heron / is on parole

gil scott-heron / is on parole
    believe it
gil scott-heron / is on parole

we last saw gil tryin to flee the country
the revolution was packed flat
between powdered bank note wads
claustrophobic / packed in his navy canvas tote

what in the hell was gil scott thinkin
with that feisty revolution hollerin
like beelzebub broke loose
oh gil / what were you thinkin
of course the cops were gonna notice you
the revolution was screamin
    lemme outta here gil scott
    i swear / progress is bein made
    ain't it progress: a black man
    headin for that white house over yonder

gil scott-heron is on parole

> *lemme loose godammit gil scott*
> *i wanna witness it*

the revolution said

> *believe it*

gil scott-heron is on parole
> *believe it*

gil scott-heron
> *oh yeah: parole*

> *shut the fuck up*

gil told the revolution
> *cause brother that false bravado*
> *is tired and old*

> *revolution*

gil scott-heron is on parole

kanye / elephunk
and missy feat timbaland
are somehow all involved
and a new cradle full of brown kids
will finally be allowed a soul
cause brothers and sisters

gil scott-heron is on parole
he's sorted out his shit
and all last night was in his studio

glory be

all our sons and daughters
can now swing low / hold on tight
little pickneys / cause here comes brother gil
to carry y'all home

lift needle from the turning table

    revolution

hush the crowds
and mic the phone

    revolution

bring the djembe snorin in the store room
and please somebody
dust off the throne

gil scott-heron is on parole

ain't nobody heard the news

    revolution

gil scott-heron is coming home

if: a rewrite

if caliban
had his homeboy othello's back
he woulda said *jesus brother*
don't be such a coconut
and that desdemona
man / what the hell
is that freaky broad about

he woulda said
i got one thing
to say to you brother and that's:
be black / baby / be black

they woulda bumped fists
and dealt crack cocaine
to hamlet / till that
erratic cat's world
was looking up

if caliban had left the island
he woulda / sold ophelia hip-hop
mercutio woulda busted a cap—
ulet in juliet's hood / like
a plague on both your house—

if: a rewrite

music would be the food of revolution
if caliban had anything to
say or do about it / miranda woulda
kicked ferdinand to the kerb
and brought screaming creole babies
back to europe

that father of hers / well
he woulda just had to
deal with it

if caliban and notorious big o
thello had ruled the town
they woulda taught that
sour shrew to break it down
in kepper pantaloons / from
two households / both alike
in brown / in some slum ghetto
where we lay our scene

it's a rewrite / but
baby / i can dream

if: a rewrite

caliban woulda fingered
the merchant's bling
soweto style / with a
12 inch 35 / to the old man's chin
he woulda drove by goneril's
and hooked up with *cordeishia*
his bootilicious queen

and king othello / he
woulda smiled / from the
royal sidelines / thinking
man / i'd give my throne
for all that hipness
to be mine

if caliban had left the island
he woulda / sold ophelia hip-hop
mercutio woulda busted a cap—
ulet in juliet's hood / like
a plague on both your house—
music would be the food of revolution
if caliban had anything to

if: a rewrite

say or do about it / miranda woulda
kicked ferdinand to the kerb
and brought screaming creole babies
back to europe

i is the revolution

your transaction has been processed by paypal
this purchase will appear on your credit card bill as
item: revolution
number of items: 1
cost: $AUD priceless

the revolution thanks you for choosing itself

the revolution is downloading onto your ipad
and being transferred onto your iphone
it is an iRevolution
the revolution is i
i is the revolution

the revolution is available in ebook form
the revolution's full text is available for 99c on amazon
the revolution comes in 4 short podcasts
that can be worn as a usb bracelet
the revolution has been turned on
you must follow the revolution
it will be abbreviated to fit its own twitter feed:
the revolution will drop all vowels / capital letters
    and apostrophes

I is the revolution

and present itself in short profundities of 140 characters
   or less
join @the revolution as it LOLs and WTFs
the revolution will have a GSOH / as
the mo fo moves in
& takes over cyberspace

dig the revolution:
take out a sub

the revolution's RSS feed will bitch-slap your inbox
every night at around about 12 o'clock
do not reply to the revolution
do not trash the revolution
the revolution is not spam
you cannot <u>click here</u> to unsubscribe to the revolution
do not drag the revolution into your junk mail can
you cannot RTS the revolution:
the revolution is anonymous
the revolution lives nowhere
the revolution is every return address
forward the revolution to everyone you know:
the revolution is a virus no norton has an anti for
infection is the revolution's cure

i is the revolution

befriend the revolution
graffiti the revolution's wall
the revolution invites all 500 million fans
to the facebook event of itself
rsvp to the revolution's event
it is the revolution: show yourself attending

the revolution will remind you of itself by SMS
the revolution has a silent number
but you can forward the revolution on by text

to find the revolution
type: revolution
into your GPS

give the revolution its own ringtone
do not turn the revolution off
the revolution must be able to reach you at all times
and at full volume

download the revolution's soundtrack
from itunes

i is the revolution

the revolution is here
the revolution is real
the revolution is now
the revolution does not exist in second life
the revolution has just been wiki leaked
the revolution is i
i is the revolution

in karikatur australisch deutsch

i
wenn ich was acht years alt
my gymnastic teacher
at epping YMCA
a schmal seriös german frau
with close-cut flames of
fuchsrot braun hair
and a favorit tabelle tennis paddle
with which she like to schlagen us
sanft / yet just that little bit too firmly
frowned at me on the double-bars
and anweisen / in no uncertain terms

> *you*
> *the black ein*
> *biesen steppen die bottom in:*
> *tuck your behind in*
> *behind you*
> *little girl*

sometimes
i scrutinise mirrors

in karikatur australisch deutsch

in the sweaty changing raums
of cheap department stores

> *tuck your behind in*
> *behind you*
in miserabel deutsch

> *this is not a poem*
> *about child abuse*
das ist just a dichtung
about a schmal braun girl

ii
at age eleven
behaviour that might have
in kindergarten
been seen as mis-
guided or understood
can be a strong indicator
for psychotisch tendencies
in adulthood

in karikatur australisch deutsch

years later
missing familie parakeets
are found
dismembered
beneath the floorboards
of a child molester's boyhood room

in klasse funf
a child who sat right
at the back of the klasse
—geographisch und academically—
a boy whose name
has long since flown
my memory
started a new game
a theater he only played
with me

> *this is not a poem*
> *about child abuse*
> *hey blackie*
> *hey blackie*
> *hey blackie*

in karikatur australisch deutsch

he would launch soggy papier
spit sache
at my schulters
across the desk
into my hair

for almost a week
the whole klasse
fixed eyes to the front
so steadily / i
honestly believed
even the kids who liked me
couldn't see / or
hear a thing

> *hey blackie*
> *hey blackie*
> *hey blackie*

i weathered the hail
for four days
before deciding to tell the teacher

> *eventuell / das ist a dichtung*
> *about a child abuser*

the teacher / angry
asked me why i'd left my chair

> *hey blackie*
> *hey blackie*
> *hey blackie*

when i explained it to her
she lachte
behind her hand
und said
> *well i guess*
> *that's what you are*

she was the teacher
and therefore
sie war right

> *das könnte eigentlich*
> *be a poem*
> *about child abuse*

in karikatur australisch deutsch

this might be a poem about the child
my teacher once was
and how those early tendencies
break through

years later
missing childhoods
are found
buried
beneath bureaucracy
in a primary school lehrer's raum

das ist nicht a poem
about child abuse

das ist just a poem
about a boy whose name
has long since flown
my memory

and a brand new game
he einzig played
with me

iii

at fourteen
i spoke / loudly
between the third and fourth
quadratic equations
of a forty-seven-minute study block

in the chalk-duster quiet
my mathematik teacher happened
to be speaking / as well

i was reprimanded
with ruler-slap
sharpness
but sir had nicht forgotten
my transgression / by lunch bell

> *this is not a poem*
> *about child abuse*

this is just a poem
about a talkative teenage frau

in karikatur australisch deutsch

sir / in smug intoxication
two terms fresh
from his
zertifikat von education
placed a tissue-thin rectangle
of loose-leaf A4
on the grafittied yellow desk
filled two entire lines
with loopy black cursive

that said:
> *i am a nuisance*
> *and a hindrance*
> *to the work*
> *and education*
> *of others*
>
> *(biesen steppen ze bottom in*
> *little girl / tuck your behind in*
> *behind you)*

smiling down
at me / sir said

in karikatur australisch deutsch

you will copy down that sentence
ninety-nine times

do you comprehend

das is nicht a poem
about child abuse
this is not a fiktion
in the end

decades after i wrote those words
behind these thin-skinned adult's lids
sir's words still scratch
like crow's feet
toward the shifting right-hand margins
of inner childhood reach

neunzig seven
neunzig eight
neunzig neun times

(in karikatur
australisch deutsche)

in karikatur australisch deutsch

> *tuck your behind in*
> *behind you*
>
> *beisen steppen*
> *little girl*

iv
several days before he disappeared
without apologie or warnung
my father scratched
the schwarz curls that
forested his chin
stared / sombre
at sechzehn year alt me
und still und heimlich
he said

> *i am going to tell you something*
> *a black woman*
> *should not forget*

in karikatur australisch deutsch

it will not ever be enough
to be as good as them

if you want to stand on even ground
you need to be much better

mein pater / with his
secreted / gelbblond
australisch frau

not a week before
he left us

mein pater / er war also
ein mathematician
in guard / of ruler
sharp precision

in karikatur australisch deutsch

v

> *dast is not ein dichtung*
> *about child abuse*

i've been clear enough
about that

das ist just ein poem
about ein mathematik fakt

when i was eighteen
> *wenn ich war achtzehn*

the student advisor
> *die student berater*

at my high school
> *in meine mittelschule*

asked me
> *angefochten mich*

what are your plans for life
> *was ar deine pläne für biografie*

struggling to lower
her eyebrows / she toyed
with her costume jewellery

when i mentioned
universite / the frau laughed
behind dubious eyes

> *biesen steppen ze bottom in*
> *schmal braun frau*
> *wert do you think*
> *si are?*

vi
at graduation
the school principal clasped my hand
against proud yellow camera flash

the auditorium was rowdy
i could not hear a thing
but at the time / i could imagine
that this is what he said:

in karikatur australisch deutsch

you are a nuisance
blackie / and a hindrance
to the work and education
of others

biesen steppen ze bottom in
little girl / tuck your behind
in behind you

this is not just a poem
about a small brown girl

(let me give you a word of warning)
das ist actually ein poem
from die valedictorian

jack

the short one stroked his silver beard
crossed sherry thin legs
smiled across the room at me
and said *so / you want to write poetry*
the other's smile curve was cut
by the thick clay rim
of his rust-coloured coffee cup
i was seventeen and yeah / so what
i was there to see about being a poet

but all a sudden i was jack / climbing stalk
all a sudden i was jack
crouched on bare knees beneath the table
jack in the giant's den / jack
with all that fe fi foe (and the fine hairs
in their jenolan nostrils curling) fum
i was jack / and the villain's wife
was winking cause damn / that woman
knew exactly where i was

so / he said / *we hear you want to write poetry*
and what i wanted to say was
yeah / i got my eye on your li'l' ole hen

jack

but i was only seventeen:
jack / off to market
with the only friend i had
and her jersey brown eyes were saying
magic beans won't keep you warm
c'mon / take me home jack
fear breathing through flared wet nostril

what kinda friend was i

i was jack / one hand a-pat the bovine's hide
and those red-rimmed eyes rolling toward me
like: *oh jack / if you could only know*
how much i love you

i was jack / all straw hat in hand
a simple farmer's boy saying
one day i'll buy you back
my friend / i promise

as cow heaved sighs
and licked at the cracked leather boots
around my trembling ankles

i was seventeen
and there to see about being a poet

but all a sudden i was jack

saying *okay then mister*
hands warm around those beans

little michael

dear michael / would you believe it
congress stood for you today
and not just the coloured section
the whole goddamn fucking chamber

you might have guessed by now mike
that jesse jackson made them
but i swear / for real / we heard
no whisper of objection

oh michael / it was the least we
all could do / sixty seconds
quiet / for lifetimes
of what we did to you / oh
little michael / who brought salvation
back / little michael
witnessing the streets
jehovah come / in a five-inch afro
and size ten bell-bottom jeans

we all shook our heads
and stood for you / little michael
silent / not knowing
it was the worst thing we could do

little michael

cause all your life folk stood around
and watched / *here comes little michael*
everybody shh check out
what he can do

oh / michael / would you believe it
today congress stood for you
same old little michael / nobody
spoke / we found gabriel in
that voice of yours / and looked past
the empty eyes

childhood locked up / behind a thug
on a tour bus / nobody spoke up
so little michael / a tired twelve-year-old
sold vinyl

well how about that
everybody was saying
little michael / y'know
that small black kid with the hair
cute smile / he sings that song ABC
and something else about salvation

little michael

dear michael / congress stood for you today
and not just the coloured section
the whole goddamn fucking chamber

mali

mali / the truth is
that we walk death row
before we learn to crawl:
a brown boy standing proud at five
is nothing short of a miracle

nine months i carried you
scared out of my mind
birthing a black child
into this world
wasn't smart / on any footing

like dumping osama in abu ghraib
and saying *have fun boys*
nobody's looking

i felt sick
every time i felt you kicking
trouble was brewing
that was no delusion / truth was
i harboured a wanted fugitive
only a matter of
tick tock tick tock

mali

matter of time / before
somebody knew

and then you're shot down
on the tube / for wearing a back pack
seven holes / not one sniper
stopping to think / that
maybe a mama was losing her child
somebody's dadda wouldn't play miles tonight

who gave the directive to shoot on sight
as if seeing was believing
and a blink wasn't worth a black man's life

mali / you weren't unwanted
everybody wanted you

the taliban wanted to strap a bomb to your back
cops wanted another black boy for target practice
hoods wanted to smoke you on the street
the street wanted you to peddle crack on her corner
rap wanted to bling you into being its gangster whore

nobody said / but i knew by the
boom shake the womb
you would be a boy

your dadda said
chill out / these are different times
you're behaving like it's 1965
but when i looked in his eyes
all i could see were whites

nobody ever spat
called him a kaffir
wrote *go home nigger*
in his maths book
said the job was taken
when they saw him coming
butchered his ears
and said the drum drum drumming
of another world was nothing

you're not free cause you're born
down under / believe me
race is race

mali

cause it will beat you
anywhere

mali / nine months
i carried you scared

the truth is that we walk death row
before we learn to crawl
a brown boy standing proud at five
is nothing short of a miracle

marngrook

back when songlines hummed
a way through grey-gum
(which was not yet called grey-gum)

back when spirits spilled
from salty inlets / that i
have no traditional name
or right / or tongue for

way dreamtime black
before the bloodshed

there was marngrook:
gunditjmara game ball

it was a warrior's sport of
thought / stealth and speed

marngrook

barefoot winged brown bodies
stretching so high through the sky
legend says / some of those
men / could fly

marngrook

before football
there was *marngrook*

it made wise men / and warriors
of the boys of this land

and this land is not mine
but if i understand
marngrook
there were also games
the white men took / and
changed / in my land

400 years ago
someone with my blood
and my fire / and my face
who gave birth to someone
who gave birth to someone
who gave birth to someone
who gave birth to me
was chained and stolen too

i do not know the name
of the game that *she* played
but i want to say *marngrook*

marngrook

when the national anthem plays
and i'm high up in the bleachers

i watch those men
whose blood is land
i see them stand heart
under hand / and sing
i see / the flicker in their eyes
watch their chests rise up
and down and wonder
how anyone in this stadium

can breathe
> *australians all let us rejoice*
> *for we are young*
> *and free*

as if it's not enough
to stand on stolen land / and sing
in joyful strains

as if it's not enough to play a stolen game
before the colonisers who deny its name

as if it's not enough

marngrook

a thirteen-year-old child
decides to really put you
in your place

it's may 26 / 2013
the indigenous round of the afl
the sun is shining / the stands
are packed / the stadium
is awash with red

white and black

at the end of this match
sydney will have wupped collingwood
by a mammoth 47 points

it's 136 in the fourth
sydney 96 to 54
goodes is heading for the boundary line
6 lean foot / of 2-time brownlow
4-time all australian / proud
indigenous swan

it's 20 years after winmar
lifted up his shirt and pointed

at his skin / in the indigenous round
dedicated to him / and goodes
hears a voice echo / in the wind
    ape / aaaaape
the voice says
and goodes turns / strides
to the front row / and points

and a thirteen-year-old child
is disgraced before the country
and the country sees its own
thirteen-year-old face

and the world is broadcast
the adolescent race hate of a nation

my children are playing lego
on the lounge-room floor

and the game is still rolling / but i
can't bear to play this / anymore

i don't want to belong
in a country of people / whose
ancestors slayed half-continents

but who still can't understand
that ignorance *is* hate

i don't want to be part
of a generation of parents / teaching
their children to *un-know*
what it is to point
to a black man and say *ape*

i want to know the black nation
that could raise a man of such mettle
he could point these cold facts out
in the harsh light of day

to a braying
marngrook
stadium

the commentators have always said
it is football
we / don't know a thing
about this so-called
marngrook

the commentators started saying

> *how can a thirteen-year-old child / be*
> *held responsible*
> *when she does not even know*
> *what it is / she did*

the commentators / they are raising
our thirteen-year-old kids

the commentators gave us new
aussie rules / and now a game
that made wise brown men
of young brown boys
can also crown kings
from fools

the truth is: we are
only ever as much
as what we teach our children
and so many of our children
have got it wrong

ask the child / does she know
about marngrook

marngrook

nuh uh
marn what

but every son and daughter
has a club / and a scarf
and a song

we are what we teach our children
and our children / are wrong

shame

if adam goodes taught us anything
on that field / on that day
it's / no matter who we are / no matter
where we are / no matter who
or how many / are watching

it is always *marngrook*:
gunditjmara game ball

it is our
responsibility
to point

megan

i hadn't seen her in five years
which seemed crazy
but in defence
she hadn't seen me

we had our heads down to the life grind
eyes steady on the grand prize
of just trying to survive
you know how life can be

but sometimes
when i was fed up / tired out / ticked off
soaked to the bone at the bus stop
smashing the snooze on my alert-not-alarm clock
my mind conjured megan
5'9" and intent on stretching
fawn hair shaved to translucent skin
because to her *beauty was nothing but a construct*
that she chose to deconstruct even though she was it

megan / who said it *was a state of mind / being free*
that we would topsy-turve the world
cause we'd invented both peace and anarchy

till i backed down / bought out / bottled bravado
and plain old stopped believing

i said *megan*
she said *hi*
like she'd been waiting by the phone
was still wild / and i was caught
in the wilderness again

her hair was knotted
still trying to deconstruct
but when the clouds moved
her pistachio eyes lit up
and my god
she had her hands full
pushing beauty back

it grew late
and over thickshakes
and stale cake
in a deserted kyogle café
she said *it's eating my cervix away*

megan

i hadn't seen her in five years
which seemed crazy
but in defence
she hadn't seen me

we had our heads down to the life grind
eyes steady on the grand prize
of just trying to survive
you know how life can be

mistah school teachah

mi teachah seh *who ye favourite poet?*
mi seh *benjamin zephaniah*
teachah seh *mi nah askin yu*
mi raise hand seh *benjamin zephaniah*
teachah seh *cheeky wait ye turn*
mi seh *benjamin zephaniah*
teachah seh *benjamin wha?*
what im bout when im at home?

benjamin zephaniah / repeat it
benjamin zephaniah / seh again
benjamin zephaniah / write it down
benjamin / mi seh *ben-ja-min*
benjamin z

look / mistah school teachah
it nah personal but / listen up
get dem white hand-a babylon
off dis feisty brown girl education
is enough!

mi blood boil / vein pop outta mi fore
head / scream hot mi mind a-fire

mistah school teachah

teachah seh *sit downg / get off de desk*
mi gwan stage it up / kick off a riot
mi back im up against de blackboard
point de chalk right at im throat
udda hand rip up im oxford best
dat keats in pieces all a-throw

benjamin zephaniah / repeat it
benjamin zephaniah / seh again
benjamin zephaniah / write it downg
benjamin / mi seh *ben-jam-in*
benjamin z

*look / mistah school teachah
it nah personal but / lord
get dem babylon white hands
off-a dis angry brown girl education
is enough!* mi seh again

den preach mi / linton kwesi johnson
consume mi / robert nesta marley
screech mi / de watts poets
beat mi / de last poets

mistah school teachah

baraka / def jam / giovanni
call mi / wanda robinson
berate mi / saul and soul nah sham

mi raise hand seh *benjamin zephaniah*
teachah seh *cheeky wait ye turn*
mi seh *benjamin zephaniah*
teachah *seh benjamin wha?*
what im bout when im at home?

nothing here needs fixing

i
at various times
after my daughter was born
my mother would say
> *sleep while the baby is sleeping*

> *sleep while the baby is sleeping*

she'd call / sing-song insistent
in that no-nonsense
west indian woman way
of us all

> *sleep while the baby is sleeping*

it was quite some time
before i realised / these words
were not about shut-eye between feeds

> *sleep while the baby is sleeping*

wasn't saying what it seemed
    but
as well as we bear our children

us women / must also learn
to dream

ii
in the middle of everything
is the eye
of the storm:

before *the discussion*
and centrelink forms
the conversation with the bank teller
and maternal health nurse's warning

before finding a house
and elaborate lies
on real estate forms

the trying to make a home
to find you have nothing to fill it with
to realise despite bare walls
and no kitchen table
the place is so full

with just you
and the kids

before school-yard talk
and determined shows
of mother strength

there is just
    the leaving
and you

that come-what-may
bittersweet / brief
heartbroken moment

where you see the light
beneath the door

and for the first time
in so long

the future
feels
good

iii
the experts are always saying
men and women
tend to grieve
differently

i traipsed
up and down the neighbourhood
for weeks

my son had just started school
baby getting on now:
ten kilos strapped
finger-sucking to my chest

men and women grieve
in different ways they say

but never
whose way
is best

myself
i missed
inspections

the bus was late
sometimes the owners
or real estate agents
didn't show
or care

often / the murmuring
weight / i carried
was just too much
to bear

men and women
we grieve
differently

i took a small unit
two streets away
on blenheim street

nothing here needs fixing

too-yellow walls
in the kitchen

elsewhere
baby blue

he said
we can't afford it
when i executed
the lease

men and women
you begin to see

how differently
we grieve

iv
lot said
don't look over your shoulder darling
god said don't look over your shoulder

but lord
she'd left behind
more than bricks and mortar

beneath the backyard olive tree
lay the ghost of a baby daughter

keep walking
don't look over your shoulder
keep walking

in the end
of course
they warned her in vain

and now we all know lot's wife
we all learn lot's wife's tale:
how she disobeyed
glanced back
and turned to salt in god's wrath

but we don't even know
her name

nothing here needs fixing

lot's wife
don't look over your shoulder
lot's wife

she'd walked free
but the smell of burning flesh
was on her tongue
it rained ash
she choked back smoke
and screamed
lot / i can't run

don't look over your shoulder
darling

lot / i can't run

and as she turned
and saw the melted screams
on the bodies of friends she'd held
while breathing
she said:

lot / if this is god
i can't believe

hers was never
a question of faith

the truth is always
worth the price you pay

so when he said
don't look over your shoulder
keep walking
she turned

when he said
don't look over your shoulder
lot's wife / she turned

she could not run
and let her city burn

nothing here needs fixing.

v
when the smoke has cleared
and the ground stops shaking
people you know stop by to look
at the charred and dust-covered remnants

they stand and stare
and shake their heads
but don't seem surprised in the least

blind love built a house
on the fault-line cracks
but they visited you there
for years

never questioning why you built there
or giving you a clue
never pointing out the shifting walls
the slant in the garage roof

and now when the ground
has stopped shaking

and the ash
and smoke has cleared

they come

with mops and brooms
and bandages
searching for you
       and the kids

vi
fingertips
trail staggered height notches in
wooden door frames furtive biro scribbles at
knee height weed-ravaged remnants of kitchen
garden faded daffy duck stickers on the
spider-cracked porcelain
       empty houses are living albums
       they tell it all
paw prints in the bathtub
kid prints on the built-ins pushbike
tyre marks on the driveway stray chewed tennis ball

under hills hoist dirty sand pit in knee-high dandelion
yard
       empty living
       leaving houses
       albums all

dog-eared child as humpty still taped to
dumpty blue
       bedroom wall

hair dust skin nails used colgate
floss wound filthy round the bathroom drain
plastic piglet spoon lost between the counter and the
oven sticky
love note not sticky any more tucked inside
a grimy kitchen drawer
       empty houses are living albums they
       leave it all
marvel comic card tucked behind a skirting board fat
sultanas secreted beneath a raised carpet
corner metre-long cobwebs whisper
       empty houses are
staggered fists marks furtive
       albums

        in plaster walls
lost
        between the counter and the oven   tucked
behind the skirting board

dog eared
weed ravaged faded staggered

spider
cracked   dirty

chewed empty
        houses
faded fingerprints

dust

        several millimetres thin

vii
the one thing you never counted on
is how hard it is

nothing here needs fixing

to be a woman alone
let alone a black woman
alone with kids

*let me alone
and get on with your business*

how hard it is
to rent a house
in the neighbourhood of your child's school
or get a job working
the hours you now need to

for five years you paid off joint plastic
and now that same bank manager
talks right through you
*you have no ascertainable steady income
i am very sorry
we just can't give a credit card
to you*

how hard it is
to get a break
or a loan

or a smile
or a hearing

or the real estate to repair
what so urgently needs mending

your child is the brightest boy in class
behaves besides
but now / they are always watching
waiting for him to slip

let my child alone
and get on with your business

a woman alone
let alone a black woman
alone with kids

the one thing you never counted on
was how hard it is

viii
some nights
i boil the kettle
then set cups
for two

ix
my wild thing children
bewitched by daylight savings
fang up at the moon

x
the new owners
live four doors down
a polite lebanese orthodox family

> *we are just down the road*
> *three doors away*
> *i am always there*
> *in the kitchen*

> *if you ever need me i mean*
> *you and those lovely kids*

i thank a god i don't believe in
the day i sign the new lease

the electric company
flicks the current
a week before
we move in

the stove-top
griller
oven
gas heater
television
nothing works

> *i don't know*

the landlady says
floured handprints on apron
cold eyes fixed on me
> *we took pity on you*
> *and now you want*

nothing here needs fixing

> *to make all this trouble*
> *about fixing tiny little things*

xi
there is nothing here
needs fixing

black-eyed pea monday nights
jamaican bun
spiced rice pudding
mild mama love
jerk chicken
and coconut rice

but on friday nights
we wing it
in fish finger
tinned spaghetti
and oven-chips style

cause isn't tiredness
a single mother's way
of life

nothing here needs fixing

love lives here
though things are tight

if these walls could talk
they'd stand tall and say
there have been dark nights
and even darker days
but only tenderness
was ever spoken

things are tight
but love lives here
if these walls could talk
they'd stand and say
this home was never broken

look around
i steer a second-hand
hand-made
home-baked
and *obedient* ship

children should be heard
not silenced

nothing here needs fixing

but both kids must be in bed by six
and just somebody even
think about giving *me* lip

broken home

nuh uh

there is nothing here
needs fixing

plantation rumour

an ole man cuts cane
an ole man cuts cane
under hot jamaican sun
back bent double
body doubled down to the ground
and all among the sugar cane
the workers whisper
see im dere
mi hear im used te be
an edukayted man
back bent double
body doubled down to the ground

five hundred lift them scythe in unison
and the sugar cane rumour mill
logs into overdrive
with its back bent
back bent double
body doubled down to the ground

a large woman
middle aged
with a horse fly drinking at the brow
say *mi hear im read fe law*

plantation rumour

inna ingland
professorship in oxford 1989

and then she shave the sugar stalk
with a quick flick
of an aching wrist
chop it up
and she stack it on the pile
before she back bend
back bend double
body doubled down to the ground

a young man
face smooth and clean
like him only just weaned
from his mama's teat
say *mi granfadda knew de man*
inna kingston school
before im grew too big
fe im docta marten boots
im laas seen
headin fe union jack atta run
but yere im is

plantation rumour

ole man body doubled down
in de dung

but the ole man cuts cane
the ole man cuts cane
under hot jamaican sun
he been all over
ain't no country else he gwan run

five hundred lift them scythe in unison
and the sugar cane rumour mill
logs into overdrive
with its back bent
back bent double
body doubled down
to the ground

ryan gosling and the new feminism

according to
sunday life magazine
as much botox as you like
swooning over ryan gosling
#extendedhashtaggingaboutryangosling
stalking ryan gosling
and *being* ryan gosling
are all exercises of female choice

and therefore
an integral part
of the new feminism

this new improved feminism
is just like the old
tired feminism

only now
to everyone's great delight

we have extracted
all the pesky feminism

leaving only
two life-affirming things:
as much botox as we want
and ryan gosling

sewn shut

every beautiful / black
sewn-shut woman
in bitter black history
i / lose control
lose my mind
love like this / for you
come curve on top of him
and we will free madagascar
through the tropic of capricorn
sisters with my
eyes / ears / airs / anger
stare down at this man / in wonder

lose control
lose your minds
break circumcurse taboo

every beautiful / black
sewn-shut woman
in bitter / black history / i

make love like this
make love like this

sewn shut

make love like this
for you

drift gently
through the mozambique
channel / girl
tanzania / uganda / sudan

let nile-wet thumb-tips
tremble dark thighs

come follow my blood-scent
through chad

for every beautiful / black
sewn-shut woman
in bitter black history
i / will love this man
love this man
love this man
like mad

show me a girl, at five

i remember / where i was
the moment i heard
she had breathed her last sigh

i was putting out the garbage bins
the children were running
round the yard
my next-door neighbour
leaned over the fence / and said
have you heard
maya angelou just died

i stood there / trying
to blink back tears
and still my trembling mouth

thinking about that warm
trembling body / born
some eighty years ago
in the violent and volatile south

at five years old
maya angelou had seen
more trials and trivialities
than most

show me a girl, at five

when she was six years old
a grown man snuck up
and almost crushed her soul

and for the next six years
maya angelou / she
did not speak one single word

one pulitzer prize nomination / one
spoken word tony nomination / three
spoken word grammy awards / seven
volumes of autobiography
when maya angelou found
her voice / she inspired
generations of fierce brown women
to speak

this year my daughter maya lou
will turn five / they say
show me a child at five
and i will show you the man

me: i want to see the mayas

show me a girl, at five

bring me all the little word-loving brown girls
whose mamas also gave them her name
so every time we called our daughters
we would be inspired

they say show me a child
at five / but i want to see the mayas

in pink-stamped gumboots and purple glitter
fairy wings / wearing
osh kosh b'gosh overalls / or
threadbare hand-me-down jeans
with high afro-curled haloes
and long coconut-oiled plaits

show me all the little
word-loving brown girls
in terracotta mahogany cedar
cream and black

let me line them up along the stage
and say *my daughters*
we are all already gathered

show me a girl, at five

and listening / and ready
to raise a whole generation of mayas

let me christen them along the line
novelist journalist memoirist playwright poet

there will be one little girl
right down the end
fists curled / knitted brow
smaller than all the rest
who will say *lady*
you just can't drag us all up here
like this / without asking
and in the middle of the night

let me point to her / and declare
amazonian literary giant

twenty years from now
we will watch on cnn
as she receives
her man booker prize

maya angelou is
every single little

show me a girl, at five

word-loving brown girl
who will not die

when i was fourteen i stumbled
on a poem / it was by a woman
her name was maya angelou

she *told me*
quite unequivocally
that *i* would rise

show us where you're publishing

this thing is
i have been writing some
and if so inclined
could mic some words across
and blow your fucking mind

i wrote a poem
just last night

not just anything
but one-a those
*goddamn-i-have-to-read-this-to-somebody
i-think-it-might-be-genius* kind of things

it is called *yoko was always going to be a problem*

see / i can tell you'd dig it
just from watching you digest the title

and i would like to be able
to give it to you
but here's the thing

show us where you're publishing

the centre's been looking for poets
to tour again
    where are you publishing
they're asking
    show us where you're publishing

packing bars and radio waves
doesn't seem to mean a thing
they just want to see the paper
    where are you publishing your poems
as if all that matters is print destination
not that almost a hundred people
would brave horizontal rain
to get to somewhere you're
doing your thing / on stage

i want *to give you* a poem
but i'm broke

it is that time of year again
when every godforsaken poet
in this place / comes shaking the tin
and filling out applications

show us where you're publishing

i would like to *be able* to give you a poem
but my children are hungry
and once again those folks are saying
without saying it
> *that 'thing' you do?*
> *naah*
> *don't even come knocking*

skin

some nights
i try to claw my way
out of this skin

but pull and scratch and bruise
seems i'm locked tight in

only ugly fat keloid
where my fingernails have been

speakers' corner
for muma doesa

brown woman / oh
on splintered soap-box
in breezy alley
your voice / against white wind
hoarse throat / tired eyes
and a body that beats / like
words been brewing
i know / for that whole
dark lifetime
finally come alive
brown woman / oh
and our history just
singing through you

the sober crowd / might
walk away / through / over
around / back-track past
the discomfort you
cause / those
black lips / brown woman
oh / though they / hands over ears
hearts / eyes / mouths / walk on
they heard you / oh

speakers' corner

brown woman /oh
heard you / break
through / that snatch
of sound on a
splintered wooden soap-box
in this here wide alley / amen
oh / brown woman /oh
say truth / brown woman
like you want it
all and then some
for me

subtext

when we say *i don't want to become my mother*
that isn't an invitation to laugh
thinking about your mother-in-law
and maybe the way she talks too loud
or repeats herself when she gets excited
or maybe you hate that somehow
your children love her / just as
they do you / because men
usually don't understand that to their child
that woman is *also* their mother
there is no distinction

if you listened to us you would hear / that
when we say *i don't want to become my mother*
what we are really saying is *i want to be
like my mother never had the chance to be*
or maybe even *i want to be like my dadda
never let her be / or even understood she was*

listen hard / cause when we say *i will not
become my mother* what we are really saying is
*i will leave you if you buy me a big square house
in the burbs / especially if you present it to me
like we're a match made in heaven*

subtext

we are saying *who are you* and
do you even know who i am
what we are really saying is *as bad a mother*
as you may think i am for it
my children are just my children
and not my dreams

i would've been about seven
first time i saw my mother on stage
it took me seven years / to
realise who she was
when i say *i don't want to be*
like my mother what i am really saying is
i am going to be / i will be / i am
what my mother was
before the world and his dog
told that girl to stop

and i am saying *if you love me*
then when i say i will not become my mother
listen / and be smart about it

summer

even when i'm famous
says the little boy
as they lay face up
on the red dirt one summer
cloud-watching the sky
i ain't never gonna forget these lazy days

me neither
says the little girl
winding a curl around her finger
even when i 'cept my academy award
it's gonna be here in this yard
live to america
by satellite through space

the end of the affair

poetry and i / we broke up last week
we just kind of grew apart
it wasn't him / it was me

well / ok just quietly / between me and you
it was wild while it lasted
but poetry / he got all single white male
for the last part there on me
it's true

he wanted to be my everything
i wasn't sure i still loved him like that
and needed some time to think
but poetry / he said
i am not gonna buy that let's have a break shit
poetry knew i wanted out
and started following me / everywhere
i couldn't work / or leak / or eat / or sleep
walk without him calling on me

you know poetry
at times / he can be so fucking needy

the end of the affair

after we split / i'd be out somewhere
and poetry would just happen to turn up
he'd pull that *fancy meeting you here* crap
as if he hadn't been hiding outside the house
to see where i went / all that time

i never thought it would end like this
i could see poetry and i / old
in rocking chairs together
hands wrapped around steaming mugs
reminiscing about the good times

when we first met i was always thinking
now poetry / he is beautiful
you know what i mean
i mean it was like: *poetry*
could have anyone he wanted
and poetry chose me
(not that i have low self-esteem)

people were always saying
girl / you and poetry
were just meant to be together
you are so lucky to have found each other

the end of the affair

and poetry would smile my way / as if to say
i will never leave you / maxine
we will be together always
you and me

and now
i am starting
to understand
just what that
might mean

unmiracle

his kind of gospel might not be sopho-aristophilosophy
this man might not be dream in baritone like king
or dangerous / like us black folk
all kind of thought malcolm was but never said / he
might not bring healthcare / world peace
race peace / education / unpoverty / a revolution
to his country / *this* country / the world / anyone
anywhere in fact he surely won't / he
might not even be a good father / husband
lover / leader / person who knows or hell even cares
if he's all that genuine / us folk know the man
ain't no solution but / he
lets us eye our knock-kneed sons
like *hey / maybe one day*
my boy could be the one

so every early morning late night newscast / every
can-i-get-a-witness same-old-black-shit day
i drag my baby to the screen
and make him watch the man
say his name / the boy says
obama
banana obama
obama in pyjamas

unmiracle

and he cackles / in his crazy two-year-old way
a no worries-in-the-world mud-pie brown boy
who just might be *my* president one day

the checkered crowd swells and heaves
like a living —
it is a living thing this
right to breathe like
damn / maybe my breath counts
that closing-in-of-a-noose-under-alabama-tree / that
back-bent-cotton-picking wheeze / that
diving-deeper-for-master's-pearls-until-one-day
your-body-just-won't-surface / those
cold grey lungs salt-logged
like a genesis curse

saying *will you blame us*
that when he called we heard / saying
will you blame us that when he called we heard / will
you blame us that when he called we
packed up the house / the life / the kids / the conscience

we / grabbed the cardboard / the car / the coin jar
and came running with all we had

unmiracle

we knew the man was mostly no
solution might not bring healthcare / world peace
race peace / education / unpoverty / a revolution
will you blame us / we didn't know or hell even care
was he all that genuine
that man / let us eye our knock-kneed sons / like
hey / maybe one day
my boy could be the one

we want poetry back

the messengers had children
the messengers had children
oh / greying guards at
the gates of lyric / saying
not on my watch
sonnets trained on the horizon
that's right / the messengers had children

oh / old white men
who shot the messengers
and those (some come even
young / of colour / or with breasts)
who bow to same

oh / you who killed poetry
marched pentameter poised across
the slaying fields of tongue
is a new dawn
the messengers had children
and the street poets have come
is a new dawn
the messengers had children
and those children have guns
is a new dawn

we want poetry back

the messengers' children have
become the messengers
and we / the messengers
want blood

you who guarded lined scrolls
and metaphored our distant dots with
squinting iambic eyes
but forgot to look (and after all
what kind of poet can't see behind him?)
and while you slept we scaled
back fences / braved body rot
and still twitching casualties in
a beat battalion tip-toe
across forbearers screaming bones

oh / old white men and those
(some come even young
of colour / or with breasts)
who bow to same
we want poetry back / we
are the children you
left wailing / without a backward glance

we want poetry back

oh / but when you cut down word
the roots undergrounded / and grew

and oh / *real poets* / you
did not think
you did not think / to drown
the messengers' children

what are you going to say

people / they have been writing to me
where are you / what
are you going to say / about
what just happened
about the westgate mall siege

like they think i am
the oracle
or something

oh / it is flattering

and believe me
some days i would roar
and sharpen these claws
to knifepoint / some days i
would wear this accolade
like the mane it should well be

but then i get to thinking

i might not want to know
that sixty-seven people

what are you going to say

are dead / in a shopping mall
in nairobi

maybe *they* need a poem
to make sense of it all

but just maybe / i don't
want or *have* to be the one
to write it

could be i been busy
with lots of other random
everyday things

maybe it is time i washed
the dried blood from my hands
and got the hell on
with living this blinkered
suburban existence

but nairobi is wailing
hate just reloaded
sixty-seven people
have been shot dead

while buying blouses
and books and bread

and the only weapon i have
at my immediate disposal
is a pen

acknowledgements

Thank you, as always, to my family, for supporting the most whimsical of dreams. Thank you the poetry teaching staff of my time at Wollongong University: Alan Wearne, John A. Scott and Merlinda Bobis, who also kept the door rotating with a steady visiting stream of Les Murrays, Luke Davieses and Bronwyn Leas.

Thank you to Lionel Fogarty, Oodgeroo Noonuccal, Pi.O, and all the other fiery Australian poets who comprise the inspiring protest canon of colour which exists right here on home soil.

Thank you—*thank you so much*—to the Melbourne Spoken Word community. This book would not exist without the past decade of love; the collaborations, the co-features, the weekend sessions at The Dan, The Doris Leadbetter Poetry Cup, the now-defunct *Spinning Room*, Overload Poetry Festival, POC The Mic, and the many more incredible things we made and lived together. I am, as always, so proud to have you as my first artistic kin. Yours is the fire which never dims.

My heartfelt appreciation to Rob Riel, founder of Picaro Press, who first published the poetry collections *gil scott-heron is on parole* and *nothing here needs fixing*, in which several of the poems included in this collection were first published.

Thank you to the Hazel Rowley Fellowship for Biography, which provided me with travel funds to research my family history. The suite *demerara sugar* was written during this research fellowship. I hope is it a worthy testament to Hazel Rowley's memory.

Finally, thank you to my publisher Robert Watkins, and to everyone at Hachette Australia, for taking the leap to short fiction with *Foreign Soil* and from there, another pirouette to poetry, with *carrying the world*. Thank you for your unwavering support on this dipping, swerving, joy-ride of a journey. What a rollercoaster it has so far been.

Several poems in this collection were first published elsewhere. *plantation rumours* first appeared in *Cordite Poetry Review*. *i is the revolution* and *unmiracle* were first published by *Overland*. *carrying the world* was first published by *Going Down Swinging*. Several poems from the suite *nothing here needs fixing* were published in *Mascara*. The title poem of *nothing here needs fixing* was the winning poem of the 2013 Ada Cambridge poetry prize, and subsequently appeared in *Award Winning Australian Writing 2013*. *confetti* was first published by *Peril*. *ryan gosling and the new feminism* was published in Ali Alizadeh's *Rabbit Poetry Journal* essay on political poetry in Australia. *get real* was first published in the *Emerging Writers' Festival Reader*. *marngrook* was commissioned for The Wheeler

Centre's 2013 *Show of The Year,* and appears in the football anthology *From The Outer* (Black Inc, 2016). *mistah school teachah* was first published in *English for the Australian Curriculum* (Oxford University Press, 2009). *show me a girl at five* was commissioned for The Wheeler Centre's 5th Anniversary Gala, in 2015. *speakers' corner* was written after the 2009 Emerging Writers' Festival event of the same name: 40 poets, 8 soapboxes, 6 hours, and a poetry-stunned public. Thank you David Ryding, for thinking outside the square.

About Maxine Beneba Clarke and Room to Read

Maxine Beneba Clarke is a committed writer ambassador for Room to Read, an innovative global non-profit which seeks to transform the lives of millions of children in ten developing countries through its holistic Literacy and Girls' Education programs.

Working in collaboration with local communities, partner organisations and governments, Room to Read focuses its efforts on developing reading skills in primary school-aged children because literacy is the foundation for all future learning. Since it was founded in 2000, Room to Read has impacted the lives of over 10 million children by establishing school libraries, publishing original children's books in more than 25 local languages, constructing child-friendly classrooms and supporting educators with training and resources to teach reading, writing and active listening.

Room to Read is changing children's lives in Bangladesh, Cambodia, India, Laos, Nepal, South Africa, Sri Lanka, Tanzania, Vietnam and Zambia.

As Maxine says, 'I support Room to Read because education and imagination open worlds, bring opportunity, and change lives. Every child on earth deserves access to education, and in an inequitable world, it is organisations like Room to Read which fight for the forgotten.'

For more information, www.roomtoread.org.